Feelings

Written and Illustrated by:
Kaan Bilhan &
Debbie Herskovitz (Mrs. Hershey)

I feel happy when
I get a new toy.
When do you feel happy?

I feel sad when I am sick.
When do you feel sad?

I feel tired when
I play soccer.
When do you feel tired?

I feel silly when I see a clown.
When do you feel silly?

I feel mad when my dad
says I can't have more candy.
When do you feel mad?

I feel worried when
I don't know the answer.
When do you feel worried?

I feel joyful when
I see a friend.
When do you feel joyful?

I feel embarrassed when
I accidentally wear my
pajamas to school.
When do you feel embarrassed?

I feel comfortable when
I am cozy in my bed.
When do you feel comfortable?

I feel hurt when
someone makes fun of me.
When do you feel hurt?

I feel excited when
it is my birthday.
When do you feel excited?

I feel curious when
I learn something new.
When do you feel curious?

I feel scared when I see bugs.
When do you feel scared?

I feel proud when
I fix something that I broke.
When do you feel proud?

I feel older when
I lose a tooth.
When do you feel older?

I feel frightened when
I see a monster.
When do you feel frightened?

I feel angry when
someone bullies me.
When do you feel angry?

I feel safe when
my dad hugs me.
When do you feel safe?

I feel jealous when
someone brags about
something I don't have.
When do you feel jealous?

I feel frustrated when
I can't write my 'e' so good.
When do you feel frustrated?

I feel loved when
my mom gives me a kiss.
When do you feel loved?

I feel disgusted when
I have to eat things
I don't like.
When do you feel disgusted?

I feel lonely when
nobody plays with me.
When do you feel lonely?

I feel bad when someone says something about me that isn't true. When do you feel bad?

I feel empowered when
I overcome a challenge.
When do you feel empowered?

I feel ashamed when
I don't tell the truth.
When do you feel ashamed?

I feel connected when
we share the same thoughts.
When do you feel connected?

How do you feel today?

Social Emotional Lesson Objectives

- Students will be able to describe how they are feeling and why.

- Students will be able to share personal experiences related to different emotions/feelings.

- Students will be able to identify and be aware of facial expressions and body language as they relate to others' emotions.

Tips for Conversation

- Be aware that EVERYONE has feelings and that ALL feelings are ok!

- Have your child draw how they are feeling now, what colors would they use?

- Discuss ways for your child to calm down when they get upset.

- Talk about problem solving skills for when your child is upset/when a friend is upset.

Feelings belong to you; they don't shape who you are.

Made in the USA
Columbia, SC
09 October 2024

43412982R00018